Mysteries in a World that Thinks There Are None

Mysteries in a World that Thinks There Are None

Gary McDowell

Burnside Review Press   Portland, Oregon

Mysteries in a World that Thinks There Are None
© 2016 Gary McDowell

Cover Image: "Tronc de la Veine cave,"
Encyclopédie de Diderot et d'Alembert, 1779

Cover Design: Regina Godfrey
Layout: Shira Richman

Printed in the U.S.A.
First Edition, 2016
ISBN: 978-0-9895611-7-4

Burnside Review Press
Portland, Oregon
www.burnsidereview.org

Burnside Review Press titles are available for purchase
from the publisher and Small Press Distribution
(www.spdbooks.org).

I.

II.

"The Bed, The Chair ..."

III.

Painting is a way of saying what it is like to be me living with you.

—Eric Fischl, American painter

So he who strongly feels,
behaves.

—Marianne Moore

I.

TRANSMISSION

You find in an alley
the mouthpiece of a flute.
Gossip alone makes music

and suddenly
from the pines the birds
all fly away.

You are devoted to giving
clear meaning to one movement.
The water in the fountain.

Down the fountain. Over it.
The prayer chapel
but its brick bench. Magnolias

in almost bloom. The failure
to believe in mathematics
is a failure of emotion—

you have spent
all of your free time.
Choral directors describe

the torso in terms of the muscles
of sound. Your wife paints
your two-year-old's fingernails

and the two-year-old says,
toes too! Sitting next to an anthill
feels like this. They work so hard.

And for so little. For salvation.
This is the mystery.
This is forgiveness.

Lately you've been dancing with all the other boys,
      and by dancing I mean screwing, and by screwing

I mean holding hands and sharing secrets: ants bleed
      when they're hurt, plants are capable of intent—

will grow toward a support—and love is what happens
      when a pronouncement of faith is answered

by the loins. Or: what makes soap lather? What makes
      us fall out of love? With ourselves. With each other.

What do animals call themselves amongst themselves?
      What do they call us? The gopher that lived outside

our apartment junior year, his huge eyes, brown,
      unblinking through every winter storm, how we'd feed

him—her?—we never did know—despite the local
      animal control office telling us not to, its body

so calm, its heart so disinterested—or alone—its feet
      wet and cold like snow in ungloved hands.

Soap lathers because: two long chains of atoms,
      one attracted to water and repelled by oil, one attracted

to oil and repelled by water. Running away from water,
      running away from oil, they aggravate themselves

into bubbles—hydrophobic, hydrophilic—smaller
than the air pockets between them. What's between

them then floats on what's not between them:
these years later I love my wife best. But most days

I remember you. Most days the nights are wound
in dreams. Most days I can't tell the difference between

secrets and lies: brass doorknobs disinfect themselves
within eight hours and storks rarely ever give voice.

Or: to love is to obsess and to obsess is to clamor or yell
or think in the background a whistle means *come here*.

There's a species of turtle that upon losing a flipper
will swim in circles for days until it can't anymore

and dies from exhaustion. A meteor shower, a long
lost brother, something to hold onto at dusk when

the blinds open, the windows close. What do we fear itself?
We fear that creating the miracle of otherness within

ourselves will be the end of ourselves, that to embrace
the ocean underneath what keeps us, that shawl wrapped

around our shoulders, burning at the surface, will
make mysteries of us and our mysteries. Once I saw

a video of a leopard killing a monkey, eating her, then finding
        the monkey's infant in a nearby patch of overgrown grass.

The leopard coddled it, licked its head, tipped it over
        like a doll, fell asleep by its side, ears alert. It's a wonder

any of us sleep at night knowing what we know.

LECTURE

It helps to be sixteen deep in the woods
where the bees come out of the ground
to kiss the gold cross around your neck,

and if you squint to see the moon's
outline etched in the blue, you'll know
how you feel, and it is holy,

and holy is the birds rushing what the creek
last left: the sunburned shad that didn't make
the channel, deep and rutted, what they give.

Chickadees, if faced with surviving
the cold, sing to keep themselves
    warm. In Arbor Vitae, ten years old,
I slept deep, and my legs
    sank through the mattress
until I found myself in a basement:
    the lapping of water at the door.
The remnants of sleep:
    crawfish scuttling backward
under rocks, their pinchers
    aimed at our toes. We can't
swim—the ice is barely melted—
    but we hang our feet off the pier,
touch them to the lake, dare
    each other to push off and stand
thigh-deep, and the cold hurts
    our knees, makes them drum,
stiffen like concrete. Dreams
    are overrated until they happen
to you. My wife: I love her
    because I hate her perfectly.
Once, she told me she loved me
    because after years of practice
she found she had a talent for it.
    On our first date, we played skeeball.
The carnie told us, *do not,*
    under any circumstances,
ride the Ferris wheel for more
    than twenty minutes consecutively.
Breaks are required.

Yesterday, I went for a walk,
found a skull in the grass.
        The ocular holes said
bird. The missing lower
        mandible said not bird. In my hand
the hollow weight said flying
        is not impossible.
I can't tell the difference between
        jaw and beak. Between beat
and syncopation. If I bleached
        the skull, I could sell it
as a curiosity, as a fact. I can't
        bear beginnings. Cold feet as a
metaphor. Quickly now,
        the risks. Young me wanted to be
an architect, a builder of skulls
        and ceilings, a maker of homesickness.
If I come back all human and hopeful.
        If it's only thunder that brings us in—
that songbird has a beautiful voice,
        and on the off chance it should
survive being swallowed, it's time
        it learned the art of leaving.

Let there be woman deranged made of words:
gardeners and snow-ghosts, moving lips
and butterfly-knots. Let there be.

Let there be man garlanded, houred.
Let there be up to our wrists a blind spot.
Let there be all that is forbidden:

songs of devotion, songs of mourning, songs
of fragile—kiss me in the whirling.
Let there be a cup of sugar. Let there be madly

open mouths, bone-stars, two bodies
in bed. Let there be undoing and more time.
Let there be a fever to subside, apple-picking,

the dipping of hands together, touch and more time.
Let there be a spine, a book leafed open,
selfishness. Let there be haircuts, matching

forks and spoons: the little things. The mice
that'll nest in the garage. Do you trap them—or
let there be *come, let's go inside*.

Let there be enough. Let there be. Let there be
lunch on a Tuesday. Quiet, more time,
two bodies because the world

could stand to be still sometimes,
and sometimes it never is, and so let there be wine
and pulp and singing and devour me.

A woman flies over our small town. Her son cries on the beach as piss runs down his legs. He wears a fedora too big even for his father, who is nowhere to be found, is exactly where he last remembers himself being. The father puts a hundred dollars on black or sips a Manhattan or tips a woman in a bikini or works three jobs and lives in a shack. The mother rises above the clouds and chases terns—she extends her arms like a child being taught to play airplane and kicks her feet as though the air were water.

In a shop down the beach, an old man sells wood-carved gulls, pelicans, dolphins, each piece of driftwood whittled until the wing, until the gular pouch, until the porpoise nose: sculpt away what's unneeded to unveil what's already there. What a concept: to create via omission, to fly unwinged, to work for stasis. In every raincloud a rainbow, in every young boy a zealot of taxonomy, but the woman won't yet land.

There's no difference between wind and sleight-of-hand, a turbine powered by the dammed river the next town over. They post the blast schedule so everyone knows when to cover their ears, tell folks, *Dreams are most often profound* .... About to hop into a taxi, Socrates spies the woman overhead. The driver asks him, *Say, what's that thing Freud says about boys wanting to fuck their mothers?* Socrates, catching the young man's gaze in the rearview mirror, replies, *It's not the boy or the mother you have to worry about. It's everyone else.*

The opposite of my foot: thus, the concrete.

The cinematography of milk-white snails big as campaign

buttons: their shells rustling together on the branches

of blue thistles in winds I've never visited.

The space between the image and its evidence:

the vase and its two profiled faces—not distraction,

but images on the same focal plane like an essay

on the subject itself. And the eyes: a place to rest.

You went to a costume party.
You loved at a distance.
The lack of bite marks
on your forearms and ankles.
You repeat: *And with you*.
A film about wild animals.
The art of the fugue: you spent
a little over an hour together.
And with you. You've taken
the wrong idiom, not as death
but as friend, you've failed
to include yourself. You walk
in circles—*and with you*—
until the shipwreck protects
your turpitude. To risk bad
humor—remorse. *And with you*.
Not the fear of effort, of singing
louder than your pew-mate.
Every thought a thwarted
sensation, a high note missed
low. Night means sleepless
night, when you dream the mask
you wore as the thundering
prophet. People guessed
the guy from that show or
Zorro, kind of. Instead, history
or its makings, some film
of small arrests. *And with you*.
The nearby of you weren't looking,
nothing more can be done.

The more you live, the subtle
wounds that lift you, holy,
to the blessed. The secret
to monsters is that they attract
us: intimacy—you draw the curtains—
all the parts of the body, *and always
with you*. To fail at crying is not
the same as missing the train
or pretending that the monk's
lamentations are any less sad
than the man's who sleeps
outside the library, his kingdom
the mineral kingdom and all men
have always lived with the vision
of argument, of idiots and their
misfortunes told. Obviously
a solution to nightmares,
the anxieties of martyrdom
exhaust even the most exigent
sentiment, and we keep singing:
Holy, holy, holy. *And with you.*

DECEMBER

A local river dreams through our yard,
reroutes over tops of pine trees,

their needles sharp with cold,

and fish, as they swim by my bedroom window,
turn into blood,

and I swear I hear birdsong under water.

Something about being lonely in a crowd.

The summer I turned twelve
I learned I could hold my breath

the length of the whole pool.

I stand on two legs. One, the subconscious
of the flying-dream,

the falling-dream.

Two, the snow-cloud, continuous,

all-sky-wide dream.

This mind is a selfish mind.
This is a party to which all

but all are uninvited.

The wasp nest I knocked from the awning
last June, a young boy's untied shoes:

where one prayer ends, another begins.

ON MARRIAGE AND TOO LITTLE DANCING

Between two deer the fog lifts the river
where fathers throw wedding rings after divorce.

The surge of a train that never arrives, or does years late,
between two tunnels, the cotton there,

the boy at the base of the bridge
casts his lure into where the water

pushes through. A dirge. A barge. The old
train tunnel where trains surged full

of cotton seed and apples and birch bark
and porcelain tubs. A hungry catfish will

take a lure. A hungry catfish, its body bright
and leaning into the stars crisped across

the river's nightmare surface, will burst
the water and make echoes the deer hear.

No wonder agony, no wonder what-all.
There are two kinds of people: those who eat

salt and those who love perfect endings.
Lungs for loss of breath, she misses him

and dances too little the work of beginning.
Whose fingers fit a fist—next summer's divine bend.

The Aztecs lamented. Corn, heroes,
history, the inevitability of strangers.

On horseback, one can see the range,
of mountains land horizon: envelopes.

Why wouldn't you sing the nights
until dawn? Of excess. The retributor

always gets caught. Pretending to be
unaffected does not mean you're unaffected.

For instance, a father cursing, chiseling,
gouging. A miracle. Children, granite,

eyes. For hours you forget who you are.
Fuck it, let the ship sink, you say aloud

to no one. Columbus sailed the ocean
bluebirds nest under your porch.

Can they see the sunrise from there?
No. But they can see the worms fat

on wet coffee grounds. Fearlessness
is the archer's only blind spot.

ANIMA

after David Bottoms

I dream of up-picked wind, begrudged
pines, bent-over, low like the moon in half water—
the other half. A mystery greater than blindness,
but deeper, jerks you, jerks me, but harder,
into the water, the small lake, the deepest
point, the drift. The nudged, the toward,
middle, the letting. Without, cast
and cast, I and the lake and I.
Fishing: the wasn't philosophy. Here's
an answer: pieces of simple, the aspects
of perfect vision in quiet terms—
to see yourself in a mirror—your eyes
can't conjugate or otherwise handle. Be that
color of sky, blurry like handwriting
at a distance. I don't know everybody,
but even the skeptics know that trembling
stars on the water's surface means
you better sit your ass down.

ARRANGEMENT

A buck atop the hill
on Hobson Creek Pike.
His nostrils like fathers.

Once, you chased *Good morning*
from your father's lips
and found the dying

German shepherd, all limbs
and unruly shadows of winter,
sprawled on the kitchen floor.

Now, this buck crosses
Church Road and stumbles
into the retention pond

where your father buried
the dog—and three hamsters,
countless goldfish. *A water burial*,

he said, *almost*. You feel a thought
shape: he was a good man.
You feel something like relief

but over what you're not sure.
A red wagon. That's how you pulled
the shepherd—Gipsy,

that was her name—to the pond.
You understand. The buck looks injured,
his hips not right, something

about his gait. He struggles up
the embankment as you pull
over. You disagree with yourself.

DECEMBER

The snow of not quite winter:

headlights or headlamps.

Have you ever put your ear to a tree
on a cold day
and clapped the trunk?

It echoes like stitches being removed
from a head wound.

A field mouse channels through the shallow
snow, tips of grass still visible

as the white collapses behind his
tunnel: he's just fast enough

and just warm enough

to outrun the melt.

A chapel's liminal space, windows
lit like a vase that's captured the sun:

we receive beauty as a nail receives the hammer's blow.

Snow is just heavy.

I buy my wife an odd number of roses
if I buy them, thorns still on.

II.

This is the way in, through posture. Outside, the robins
break. Define *warble* as two women, having just met:

God, you are so gorgeous. My mouth on your mouth, my mouth—
when I press my fingers to my forehead in prayer,

it's the long breeze I wait for, the hollow my mouth makes
on *Ahhh-* and before *-men.* Your clavicle under my tongue

is a runway at night: it always looks like I'll overshoot
the landing. The speed of darkness. What fears me?

Practice resurrection and predict the months, one man
orders the other men. What war was that? As a boy

I found a pregnancy test in the backyard. Two blue lines.
The baby born some months later, a goodbye knot

in my stomach, was lulled by the light and so came barreling,
red and burning of body, into the world. That baby was rocked

to sleep like any other baby, left home eighteen years later
to learn the world, and came back blooming in sighs.

COME MORNING

From the air, irrigation canals look like hands
with their fingers spread wide, stretching to palm

their fields—and also like an artery, its vascular
malformations ridged and lodged into place:

any breathing up here is done with a river's patience.
This fall a coyote, brown-backed, silver-haunched,

crossed the broken cornfield behind the highway.
The way light frames it, ghosts it bare, the color *ash*,

the flint-points of its teeth, and the boys that chase it
from the playground: they pretend to be airplanes,

engine-breaking, barking at the coyotes, and on my deck
I open the gas grill to a flutter of bluebirds,

their nesting hay trailing behind their unforked tails
as they slope back to the woods, their unborn chicks unsure

how to survive the girth of the night and will know,
come morning, cold by the coming of cold.

Thinking too hard there's nowhere to hide.
An entourage of chariots riverside.
Go, wash yourself seven times in the River Jordan.
Eyes closed but dilated but humming—
we've surrendered like a question.
The water bubbles from the ground
in the North, says the preacher, *is never*
deeper than a sapling is tall.
It's not that the dictionary works
but that the Bible helps you understand
what drowning feels like. Aram paved
the River bottom with shekels of gold:
This is My Body, just as He Said.
Every river is deep enough to wade
at dusk—every river is deep. At dusk
a grass spider weaves from the patio
table to the grill and I listen
for the rain that'll knock him groundward.
Before I sleep, I cup cold water to my face
and think how *please stand as you are able*
sounds a lot like *I prefer it this way*.
And after baptism, I still think that to drift
downriver would mean there's one less place to go.

Defined: he paints the bereaved, their cargo,

their errands, loyalties. Their shadows incapable

of themselves: what survival will involve is unclear.

And this man, at the cusp of the ocean—I'm nowhere

near him. I'm at the beginning, and I have no quarrel

with light or water or man, or the organized lying

of colors: faith without eyes. Texture: if there should

be a firm hand. I can do no better than to listen.

The difference: I'm not O'Hara, and I'm not a painter,
though I, too, wish I were—I'm also pretty sure
my neighbor hasn't vacuumed since he moved in
four months ago, and the difference between eggshells
underfoot and eggshells plastered to his latest installation
of old radial tires or Florida Orange crates is perception:
something O'Hara and I have in common. Painting
is definitional, many-tongued, forked or spooned, cut-
through and layered. I've lived in O'Hara's poem
for a few weeks now, and my beard is long, and I can't
forget *how terrible orange is and life*. Of all the circles
I've run, I like the ones where I can't tell
if I'm coming or going but I definitely know
that if I were to fall where I stopped I'd be lost
to the horizon or dimmed enough so as not to care about
the sudden rainfall filling my mouth, soaking my clothes:
and now I'm heavy. Pollock was heavy. He'd lose himself
to the booming and anger of the white water rapids only
to succumb to long trances of nothingness where blue
became the closest color to flight. His mother
beat the laundry clean against the shore,
the smack and subsequent waving of cotton in the wind,
bliss after bliss, the moment when his body shook.
Asked once if he played any musical instruments, Pollock
said, *I still tamper with the mouth harp*, and I still move like
the mouth harp, the continual pulse of the mouth harp,
the quivering to let go, and O'Hara: *yes, it needed something
there*. My neighbor, the one who won't vacuum, waits by
his front door every morning for the newspaper, coffee
mug in one hand, cell phone in the other. He snatches

the paper off his porch and slides it under his arm, just like
on TV, except there's no music, no zoom to capture
his tiny eyes, squinting, plotting. He just turns
quietly back into his apartment to make something or read
the local forecast, the lottery, the drip-drop of the crossword
puzzle. I've grown accustomed to silence, the not-art
of cracked eggshells and three-day-old coffee grounds spilled
next to the garbage can, but I can't help think of my neighbor
spying from his porch, think that maybe the installations
in his window mean something. I knock on his door.
He doesn't answer. *I go and the days go by and I drop in again.*
In his window: a bicycle tire, some tinsel, an axe, glue, paint.
So this writing goes on, and I go, and the days go on until
the writing is finished and I'm tired, really tired. Pollock, late
in his life, always painted drunk. Lee Krasner watched him
dip his cock into yellows and reds and after several shakes
over the canvas he'd fall, not flat, but perfectly.

Fire is fire
in every history.
Only its function
changes. I know
what birds are
and what fluctuates
between them. *Perimeter*
was invented by
a prophet. *Invented*
was propheted by
a poet. Fractal,
fuel, and practice:
what risks we
must take. Loose
necks bow, pretend
their baritone outlasts
whatever their vertigo
demands. When fish
swim, they make
holes in the water,
says the philosopher,
or was it
the crowd-pleaser,
the ichthyologist. One
time I found
a freezer abandoned
on the roadside:
what initial mistake
put it there,
what made me

want to pilfer
its remnants, steal
sour milk, bruised
pears, tie it
to the hitch
and drag it
ceremoniously across
this goddamned town.

The road gives off steam. All of it
evidence. Take 440, merge east to 24,

split further east onto 65, then south. The trouble
with directions, says my old man, is that

they're so damn definitive. There's no longer:
go past the third tallest pine on the left,

take the second right and follow three bends
in the road. At the abandoned paper mill,

hang a slight left. No street names. None needed.
The naming of streets came only after landmarks,

only after suburbia: the word *avenue* from "to
approach, to come," "a way of access," "how

to belly up to a country-house." To travel.
You can't go home. The natural slope, the belly

of a hill, a rusted fence, barbed wire. So much rain.
It's a religious moment the first time you step

on a northern Wisconsin pine cone barefoot.
The second time: I've already had a father,

and while one is alive, you can't have two. In Louisiana,
they ask me if I want my beer to-go. *In styrofoam,*

no one knows the difference. I order two more. One way
to measure a bass: how much of your hand

can you fit in its mouth. A creature that fears
the motion of its nest. The image of the valley

is also the image of the universe. I taste my own
body in the ocean's sand, and I remember pleasure,

as hard and for as long as I can. It's only June.
Swimming is a perfect silence. We disappear.

DOXOLOGY

A man meeting his god is another form
of night: surely they will curve back

to the river where one will say, *feed my sheep,*
feed my lambs. Do the same. You sit in the aisle

nearest the window so you can watch the parking lot
and the road, the trucks filing to the interstate—

you're careful not to think anything
that you don't already understand.

The Confessions tempt you to believe
that stolen pears are only stolen pears,

that the preacher's notes can be thrown,
like so many stolen pears, to the pigs,

but it's too late to be morning
always. St. Augustine, while in his garden,

heard a child chanting, *take it and read it*,
but the difference between a sermon

and *are you finished eating* is not the difference
between curing the spirit and planting sweet basil,

the downturned mouth and particular quiver:
all that wounds are. The woman in the pew

in front of you coughs, and the preacher
pauses, coughs himself. Contagious like a yawn,

the cough rolls through the congregation:
your health when you're sick is the body coming,

the first time. Out the window, fire engines.
Sirens are red when you hear them

from far away through stained glass.
Praise the Lord, all of you bright stars,

praise the name and the broken. Do the same.
Do the same, photos you take, though

terribly composed: the celestial blurs of light
where your fingers meet the flash. Do the same,

the story you heard about a deer and a bear,
best friends. The bear would bend down

the bough for the deer to reach the leaves:
we all reach the leaves because someone

bends down the bough. Do the same,
faith, and pluck five smooth stones

from the stream. Do the same, *I think there is no light
in the world but the world*. Do the same, when small

spiders, during a spring rain, weave themselves
out of the walls, unravel their bodies in a long curve

floorward. *And I think there is light*. Besides,
a metaphor is a knuckle without a spine.

Definition: time where time is negligent, where a fire-
ant's sting is a light bulb brushed against your skin.
Honey, be careful what you wish for because sometimes

it comes true. And then the swelling, the burn, ideas,
quick figments of a narrator, a chorus and then
a single boy. It's possible to have more than a dollar

in change and not be able to break a dollar—
so make sure, sweetie, that you always have a dollar.
We've a no-slip rug in our living room.

The point is to lose yourself completely
in bad dreams without musical accompaniment
where you know there are risks to looking out

the window: thunderstorms, aquariums, some other
kind of miracle. Your hands can shield the sun—
don't let your eyes fool you: 8 minutes takes only 8 minutes—

but you've got to move your hands: horizontally and then
south by southwest. The opera balcony you can fish from
holds a single note all night, doing what it can

to keep your eyes open. Sleep is an assessment
to make shapely your wake, so rest well, darling.
The cold snap last winter broke our thermometer.

The bees are constellations in the garden,
drunk on basil and shining.

The world needs experience,
I need two windows,

one to bring light and one
to bring—your lips are salted

like pumpkin seeds, blanched almonds—
the crickets closer. I wish I could sing.

My son practices writing his name
on the window with his forefinger.

He draws circles around the sun, asks me,
where's the moon go at sun-time?

One morning, my neighbor woke
to find a robin nailed through its wings

to his front door—its nest,
with two blue eggs nestled still,

sat on the welcome mat. *Kids*,
he said. That night we drank wine

on his porch, watched the bats
hang from the pylons like black

grapes. In twilight they gathered
themselves, and once it was pitch, lunged

and fluttered after bugs visible only
as fuzzy shapes under the streetlamps.

Now, your forehead is hot.
I feel like singing. Vines grow

up, crawl the sides of things, root
shallow and cling. *The cruelty of death*

is that it brings the real sorrow of the end
but is not the end. When it rains here,

little stones fall too, pinging
off the windows, and sometimes

off the birds. They must think
they will fly forever, in the same place.

BECAUSE I'LL NEVER BE A GARDENER

at the Chicago Botanic Gardens, August 2009

The first thing I see is the Glorybush, my son reaching
for its flowers, its purple hiccups, and I could list all the plants

on this side of the zigzag bridge—an ancient legend tells
that evil spirits move only in straight lines and cannot follow

those who swerve—but I'd rather tell how yesterday
my boy turned one, and how I believe he'll turn one again

tomorrow, and like streetlights and lovers, I'll let him turn
and turn because only yesterday my wife told me, four

years into our marriage, that white tulips are her favorite flowers.
But I haven't been killed dead yet. Last night, in the dark of her fragmented

touch and the silent pronouncement of some unfed fear,
some death like a race horse's on the track: that silence,

that in-rush of shock that makes us all human—
but there aren't any horses here, only the Sansho-en,

the Japanese stroll-style garden of three islands. And we walk.
In Japan, age is strongly revered. Young pine trees are trained

to give the illusion of age: front branches removed
to expose the shape of the trunk, rear branches tied down

so they appear weighted by time. Foliage is pruned
each year to slow growth. I can't help but read the placards

below each plant and flower, the funny captions,
the unpronounceable Latin names, the insignificant facts:

to keep zinnias all summer long, deadhead
the flowers after bloom. They are drought tolerant.

Zinnia elegans: Ruffles yellow. The lance-shaped
leaves of the Sawtooth oak, the *pop* of its cup-enclosed

nuts. A list of what I've seen is akin to describing
a painting brushstroke by brushstroke, each color

broken down to its elements, the fragrances
of freshly stretched canvas, the teak or sheesham

mango floater-frames that keep the paintings
from blooming across the whole room.

The sunburned view, overheard—just plain quiet.

How like brigands we are, living on silence and

a long walk on air. A voice speaking above a whisper.

A hidden place near dawn, a place north-of-no-avail.

Our secret: we'll row to the fear of hiding: a seafaring

man knows the sound of oars close to the wharf.

Lately, I'm jealous. Of rocks,
their candor. Of war-torn prairies,
of tall-grassed prairies. Of men with nothing
but knapsacks and last names:
miles of road ahead of them,
their next stop here or there
or anywhere but here or there.
Of prayers and paintings:
I will not think like this forever:
Fischl's *The Beginning of the End*,
how simple: the bridge through
her legs, and in the clouds,
sunlight or sunset. Well, I've been
nail-clipped before, harbor-winged and cut
into a gathering of facts, of questions
and answers: swarms of bodies,
beached or tanned—it all leads
to violence, one last chance to stand
together as alpha and omega.
We've been *there* before:
standing wet and cold.
Perhaps being dragon-flied,
tit-moused, and marbled isn't enough.
Like Dante's nemeses,
we're simply *pilots of the livid marsh*,
and, in the end, that will be what saves us:
our startled wings, our weight
and shrill voices and beating hands
that eddy in our hearts like guilt
waved to empty shorelines.

But I'm only jealous lately.
Of unfurled doors, of dark-housed
eyes. Of devices spined of my own making.

The Bed, the Chair ...

... the more familiar you get with your themes, the harder it is to be lost.

—Eric Fischl, American painter

... turning.

Orchards: trees limbed,
of course. Practice preaching.
Survival of the solvent swishes,
apples pruning in the heat,
in the hear: a figure
half-turned, half-doored
and already forgotten.

       Here's the slip—
the sun and its constituents:
the woodlands,
the first time you see color—
riding on your dusk-gliding
skin is the stretch of patience
it takes to outgrow comfort.

… play.

Crossed-haired and driven, your
body like an icicle where
your teeth once were, where

your hands now are, water-faithed,
boarded, hand-culled:
a virgin if you ever slept.

A virgin if you ever woke:
lamped and wetted (and whetted),
this landscape of windows

and rolled gardens of bushes.
How to pull a bed frame
up a hill without crashing

through the countryside.

… head to foot.

So often what's in focus becomes
patience: you hip-handle him,

and in this moment the names
for things become shoeless.

The axis on which they spin
becomes unisoned—

the past, verbed into being, is not
the same thing as a microcosmic
view of thighs or a downspout,

a mysterious rain.

. . . jetlag.

Having flown this far already,
it's only fitting that half
of everything is in profile:

the welder, the obsessed blonde,
and his shade-blinded ribs
underneath a chest so large

you can't pillow your face
into him, can't light-eye
your way into hiding

between his arms and your hair.
You're lost now in blindfolds,
hamstrings, and red chairs,

but you're too tired to sit,
and those welds won't hold forever.

... touched.

In the confusion of pleasure's
matrix, even arched and widened
lamp-light can't keep

the paintless walls
from staring at the blur
between your legs. The lift-off

of sheets and hooves, the wood-
beamed door in the corner:
its circle, your bird-browed

lips and the faith it takes
to accept flying as a natural
occurrence, as a collarbone

of teeth and cogs, as a clock.

... the sitter.

Cavely lit countertops
and cupboards, their lines.
A stiff neck, the bed
framed in echoes. The chairs
and the meaning of life:
you forgive what's important.

Here are legs, crossed
and lost in themselves.
Of all the possible reasons
not to break a mirror:
hips—not in pieces,
but in fractions.

… changing.

Balance resides in the chest.
Your jump-stop.
Your head rides high—

redbirds or bluebirds: all light
blocked from stage-left,
your knee lit surgically

—foregrounded—

where all else is dark. A solo now,
dancing, each rib a new note
on a scale misnomered

because weight,

like birds on a chair, has nothing to do
with density or heft,
but everything to do
with what's immeasurable.

... waiting.

Band and trap, or vice versa.
Now, *go get 'em boy*—
the posturing of the hunt:
at rest, an endless oncoming
of whistles. At non-rest,
a cluster of fingers and bullets,

that dog from down the street,
his barking keeps
the neighborhood awake,
but when he swims after
the goose or the pheasant,
his master, gun propped on his shoulder,

colliding through the reeds,
the cold pond water sloshes
over the top of his waders,
my God that dog is beautiful,
my God, thank you God
for this meal we are about to eat.

... crossing.

No more skin, nothing
to show these hands.

Over and turn, end, turn
again: sleep comes slowly.

Things are named, sometimes
twice. Sure-footed, serened.

Bed-sheets have fingers
and snowfall is silent—

all the yodeling of insomnia.

III.

THIS SUMMER WITH FISCHL

I must repent for this summer I've spent beyond creatures,
for the mysteries I've seen in a world

that thinks there are none, a world where we've named things—
garage, fence, robin, poem—so that we can feel

something when we destroy them.
I must repent for the chlorophyll in the leaves,

the time I've spent in the pool, no raft,
my convexed back keeping me afloat,

for the hours wasted hoping the clouds above me
would form into something weighted,

so that I could be touched by something
other than a man begging for change outside the library.

I must repent for the sunflower, its aching, arcing
reach for light, for staring at the woman next-door,

her meticulous morning routine: compact the trash
in the can with a snow shovel, add a full bag from the kitchen,

return the lid to the can, and weight it with a ham-tin filled
with pennies. I too wouldn't have believed it.

Every time I turn my head to look out the window,
I see a harsh light through the blinds, striping everyone with shadows,

I see Fischl's *Bad Boy*: a teenaged boy, a purse full of money,
a nude woman (his mother?) on her bed, leg bent, arched

toward her mouth. What must it feel like to be stitched together,
thefted-after like a bowl of apples and bananas in a Freudian dream?

In another painting, a woman crawls naked through a backyard,
huddles against a row of hedges. While I haven't seen that,

I must repent for the squirrel that fell from the tree,
for my dog who wouldn't let go of its neck.

The hours I spent looking at beach scenes: I repent.
The incest, the drinking, the affairs, the nudity: I repent.

The thinking beyond line, beyond shape: I repent.
I repent: the patio tomato plants, watercolors, prints,

maquettes of the neighbor's new garage, king crab legs
for dinner, a nude sunbather on her belly, her back damp,

her boombox sweating Shakira, Marc Anthony, and then silence.
The eavesdropping, the baseball on the radio, sweet peas and carrots.

For the old man across the street, his bad hips, his garbage can
that I move to the curb, his cane, too short for his arms: I repent.

In many of the paintings, I imagine a quarrel between
two lovers—or is it a monologue, a palette of yellows and reds

through the kitchen window each morning, their cups of coffee
barely settled on the counter before they begin. I must repent

for the unneighborly innuendos, the pile of dog shit
on the driveway that someone will step in, unaware that they have

until later, much later. I must repent for repenting, for repeating
myself, but this summer of recycling bins and large paper bags full

of lawn clippings has named me differently, and Fischl, his naked
eyes, have given me a hard-on for all things domestic:

gossiping, love-making, dog-walking, putting myself ahead
of myself only to find myself lost in myself, lost because

nothing is what it seems here. I must repent for spending so much
time with the mysteries of texture, with a book that weighs more

than my son, with my neighbors as if my neighbors were paintings,
as if their lives were canvassed, colored, hung on my eyelids.

The streets, the beaches, the neighbors: all starkly lit scenes,
a robust sense of everything having been played and replayed,

rehearsed like *Sleepwalker*, that skinny boy in the porch light, cock in hand.
The lawn chairs empty, and we watch him like we want to help him,

like we can touch him ourselves and make him stop, but he won't stop,
not until the lights go out or the sun rises or we fall asleep watching.

I must repent for not watching more closely the bagpipe-lined
streets, for the way the doves peck at the window when they're angry

or confused or cold or hungry. Perhaps I haven't been
completely beyond creatures. Perhaps my creatures, destroyed,

I thought, before I started here, are merely lost in the lines,
the colors, the textures of a painting I have yet to encounter.

because nature is a haunted house
because my kids are my religion

because who has time to make
ugly beautiful again, and who wants

to be known for what they didn't say
because why not, Fischl, my obsessions

aren't your obsessions, so   because
even after all these years I still can't pray

with my eyes open   because opening
my hands to grasp her pant leg

to stop her leaving   because I don't lose

pennies between the seats of my car
because constellations indeed

because we had a picnic, joined the dance
among the leaves, ate sea salt

by the pinchful   because we forgot
the tequila   because given sunlight

let's plant the pyramids: all wit and no play
because deep in the mirror this morning

a face I recognized   because

DEAR OBSESSIONS,

The first honeybees of the season will soon make
their way to my porch where last year they fed

on our marigolds before hurtling back to the tree behind
the garage, their hive skewered in the sinus of the dead

trunk. We went with marigolds because we read that bees
can't see the color red: zinnias and peonies and begonias

and the red fox that frequents our backyard, his dark winter
coat, his hollow hairs, shedding, lightening: no need to insulate

until next winter, until all over the world. In Burundi, thousands
of albinos fear for their lives: their organs and limbs

treasure-hunted by witchdoctors: their hands for healing
and good luck, their legs for wealth, their heads for freedom,

their tongues for the power to turn something into anything,
and like trying to fish in too large a lake, authorities cannot

protect the huge swathes of albinos wandering the countryside
unable to trade or cultivate their fields. And in my lake:

walleye-speak: twenty-nine-and-a-half, eight-and-a-half, inches
and pounds, my father's age and my age. How late into the night

can they see each other's eyes in the backwash of the dam,

the stillness of a deepwater hole: obsession begins and ends
with questions. I often wonder if Fischl fishes and if he does

whether he wades, boats, spear-fishes, noodles. *In painting your
hand follows your eye, and in sculpture your eye follows your hand*, he says,

and I believe him. *The Wait*, bronze, reminds me of the frustration
of prayer, the coming of warmth: *the hand feels the form and then the eye looks*

to see if it looks the way it feels. Juncos, blue jays, cardinals, and hawks:
the way it feels. Spring, though it lacks in consistency, arrives

just in time to save a marriage, in time to spawn the walleye.

*My sculptures are most successful at one-third human scale. The body is charged
at that scale, meant to be caressed at that scale*. Elsewhere, the chronic swell

of rivers, of oars the dead can lift where the restless gather at dawn:
a dam abandoned, a train whistle shaking the leaves overhead

all in scale, all in frames, all the neighborhoods and their hungry,
and in the damp soil earthworms eat their walls—the minutiae

of walls, of riverbeds cresting, and letters to family: Dear Obsessions,
I owe you an apology. Dear Obsessions, swallow whole your loose

continuous lines, your musculature. This is the way I am in the world.

The loosed strength of the deep night. Sand
buries to your shoulders—even a holy man

doesn't know the way into the body. Yellow is the sun
is a place I've known as beach. Freud once said

that everywhere he'd been a poet had been there first.
The notch of a single voice, the tick-tock of the filing

cabinet closing, birth and death of a halo: I work
when I sleep, because that's when I move inside the lust.

That I wasn't born a different animal. That I can't drink
and speak at the same time. With attached wings,

humans could fly on Saturn's Titan. With attached wings,
I love you. Immeasurable dust, we are bubbling brothers.

People who have loved me my whole life have died
and my body, heavy with sleep, insists being born is like this.

In one of Fischl's *Scenes of Late Paradise*, a man,

juts of clouds or rocks, both black against the blue sea—

and this man froths through the white sea as essence.

The grinding of empty shells and bosom swells,

the innocence of fault, like calling the ocean a pool,

a rock a pebble, a tiger a cat, a painting a picture,

or maybe a periscope pointing south, under the horizon:

its mountains and oceans—phantoms.

On my days off, I fold paper,
fold it tens of times to make the creases
stick, over (and over itself).
My fingers are nimble.
But all those sleights I spent hours
mastering (cuts, fans, double-lifts,
glides, the tenkai palm) couldn't prepare me
for the folding, the creasing of cardstock
needed to make paper fly. My palms
trained to ghost what they held,
my knuckles trained to resist showing strain,
to forgive what pushed against them,
and still I couldn't crease paper
into unnatural shapes,
into folded flying machines.
It wasn't about strength, but misdirection,
which takes a lifetime to master. Is life
more than its illusions?
I'll let someone with tonsils and bravado answer this.
(I've always found it's fair,
and right, to say, *I don't know*).
But I like what I've seen, and it's no illusion
that the beaver behind my childhood church
could hold his breath for nearly an hour,
could hide in his stream,
under his logs, and not show himself
for nearly an hour. But I knew
he was there, his dark form
shadowed by the sunlight.
He didn't need to be seen, didn't need

to hear me tell him lies, tell him
I wouldn't hurt him.
I only wanted to tell him
that I understood his life, teeth and tail,
that I'd read about him in a book once,
knew that he couldn't hide
forever. Illusion is tactile.
In this way, it's like sex or youth, death even,
or like flying a folded sheet of paper
across the room. To vanish quarters,
transpose thimbles and silks, produce
cards and ping-pong balls from air:
the eroticism of the unexpected:
to cast a shadow with my hands
over silver dollars, move them across the floor,
no strings, just muscle memory
and misdirection, the result of obsession,
the reproduction of faith, the gasps
that would follow. I will never fold
anything perfectly. I've gone to church
a few times, as a child mostly,
and from Sunday School I remember
that the animals were created when we were created,
and that only *the kindest acts of the wicked are cruel*.
Is this how we deceive each other—
pretend to see each other for what we are,
but what we are is never more
than the distance between our heads
and our fingers. I crease the paper
diagonally, hope that in flight

the pleats will hold, will make of paper
what I can make of shadow,
of a simple object held lightly in my hands.

Rocks rolled smooth by river water and rain: shadows like dead presidents' suits. The double-breasted next to the long-tailed, the three-piece. The conversation they'd have. How fear reproduces. What heart. What bend. The rocks, the flats, from shore to shore only twenty yards: the water's not so fierce. Vests and cumberbunds of trout or rocks, the dark muscles. Soaked to his thighs, the current pushes shells and pebbles under his feet. How he nearly floats upright, the water swirling around him as if he doesn't weigh.

SIMILE

Last night, coyotes circled my backyard:

a neighbor burned leaves,
smoke-clouds

shaped like teeth and jaws,

like ears, like howls riding the rooftops.

The kids at the park: *no way, dude,*
komodo dragons eat
tin cans and scrap metal.

I think you're confusing komodo dragons
with goats.

And the oak tree my son sits under:
acorns are nature's little bullets.

Isn't the view from the park
also a part of the park?

MY CHILD NOT MINE: FIRST PRESBYTERIAN, SOUTH STREET

Tonight the city is full of heavy doors.
The boys on the corner of South

and Rose play catch with a hatchet
or shuffle their feet to the honking

horns: the boys are the cars no one else
is driving. Tonight it is finally

the first cold of this autumn: the weeds
of the vacant lot have withered

since mid-summer when they stretched
toward the church, followed the setting

sun to the stone circles carved
high above on the tower, the stones cut

years ago with slow blades of harder
stones. And across the street, the Indian

burial grounds, the boys: head-dressed
or nude—or both—and the headstones

now barely darkened of the crow's
flight west over black, iron

fences, a gate adorned with goose
feathers, dried pork rinds, or cored apples

87

still red-fleshed and veined—the boys
and their seeing and their time and their

sunlight. Seeing requires nothing
but a tongue, nothing but an expired

parking meter, a young intellectual
sitting alone on the church steps, book

cradled in his hands, and suddenly
I'm a door to what I fear most: something

like headlights or mornings when I wake up
sweating, trying to lift him from my legs.

Swan-divers and ospreys ignore gravity
differently. Overhead, night clicks
as the dog sniffs one more time
the periphery. Today, the botanical
gardens: this is the pistil
and these are the stamens. Notice
how slender—they are just like mouths.
Consider the rush of clocking
the sun, the wind, how shadows
grow Cubist against the lake,
talons rounded rather than grooved,
a reversible toe. You glove your hand
with a plastic bag to clean up
after the dog. It's difficult
to prove something, especially that
which you've always wanted:
to fly, to myth, to ribcage,
to illuminate the sky as *fragile,*
creased—you've always bruised
so easily. You like to think
you've come a long way: the salt
in your cupboard, the lake hidden
there. Or smaller. The boat
you'll sail away on, the rock you'll
worry smooth. Even smaller.
Can you imagine unknotting this rope?
Thank goodness you don't have to.

SILHOUETTES

Me myself in the summer heaven, godlike, brushstroked,

swirled uncommonly large, and in the foreground

is the background: an unhappiness born by the paint

and the canvas. The good news: my silhouette

is aggressive, like a tumor on a deer. The bad news:

the deer never survives the night.

RUPTURE IS NOT TO BE CONFUSED WITH LOVE

The rain I want and the rain given   the tomato
vines crawl the side of the garage, reach the top

of the lattice, and curl downward again, heavy

with fruit   the hydraulic pulse of morning's
migratory flocks   air made ripe by bodies

the silver residue of slugs up the doorframe
and the dog licks the morning   some dark shape

her hind makes in the dawn   this is the disease
I've been told will cure me of mind and so I

begin listing: the mice flee, spread what's not
been harvested   seeds   do hummingbirds

fuck midair   how do their wings leave space
the coffee cools and the grass dries   consciousness

is an exile   deep in the woods   mockery
onions bigger than potatoes, mushrooms   oh

the clouds   turn from my lips or kiss what speaks
less   a prelude, a suitcase, a rotten avocado

my heart is beating so fast I am in the future   and next door
a gazebo   and next door   it's time to go back

inside our bodies   we can disappear only what belongs
to us everywhere   is pouring   and we call that privacy

AUTUMN TAKES INVENTORY

I have an extra pair of goggles, a grandfather
I've never met, a prehensile comprehension
of mirrors, two eyes that do adequately recognize

a leap year. I eat more when someone
else pays, and I have decided to build a house,
to expect warmth. I have moons

for a heart, drapes for drapes, and
too much kindness, so when your shoes
fall out of the helicopter, I'll fall

after them. Hello ghost, let's use
one another, let's be a face in the fireplace.
The Earth's atmosphere doesn't have an end-point

but becomes thinner and thinner until
it doesn't exist. I have the next afternoon,
a screaming child. I have immeasurable orchards.

A deep pool to swim in a single breath: the pressure
on my cheeks to hold my lips sealed. I have made
someone cry, and I'm sure I'll do it again.

"The Bed, the Chair ..." is a title of a series of Eric Fischl paintings. The poems are in conversation with those paintings.

Other Fischl references are scattered throughout the book. If a painting is mentioned without naming an artist, it's a Fischl.

"Silhouettes": The italicized line "*Me myself in the summer heaven, godlike*" is borrowed from Robert Frost.

"*I Write a Line about Orange*": Most of the italicized language in the poem is quotes from Frank O'Hara's poem "Why I Am Not a Painter."

"December": The italicized line is borrowed from Diane Seuss.

"Dear Obsessions,": The italicized language throughout the poem is excerpted from interviews with Eric Fischl.

ACKNOWLEDGMENTS

Grateful acknowledgment is made to the following journals where the following poems first appeared, some in different forms:

A Poetry Congeries: An Online Artifact: "*Holy*, from *To Cut*" and "Liturgy"

The American Poetry Review: "Rupture Is Not to be Confused with Love" and "Anima"

Anti-: "Simile" (as "Working Class")

Barn Owl Review: "December" ("The snow of not quite winter:")

The Bellingham Review: "Because I'll Never Be a Gardener" and "*I Write a Line about Orange*"

Conte: "My Child Not Mine: First Presbyterian, South Street"

Cutbank: "Repent"

Fifth Wednesday Journal: "The Beginning of the End"

Front Porch: "Doxology"

The Georgetown Review: "The Discontents"

H_NGM_N: "The Bed, the Chair ..."

Hotel Amerika: "The Painter Goes for a Swim"

Indiana Review: "This Summer with Fischl"

The Journal: "Arrangement"

The Laurel Review: "A Fable"

The Missouri Review Online: "Massive and Tiny as a Star"

The Nation: "Transmission"

Pebble Lake Review: "Simple Objects"

Qu: "A Prayer for Marriage"

Salt Hill: "First Date" (as "After Watching Hugo, I Go for a Walk")

The Southeast Review: "On Marriage and Too Little Dancing"

Southern Indiana Review: "Mysteries in a World that Thinks There Are None"

Superstition Review: "Silhouettes," "On Civility," and "Autumn Takes Inventory"

Tupelo Quarterly: "Come Morning" and "My Mother the Philosopher Considers Non Sequiturs"

Tusculum Review: "Dear Obsessions,"

Zone 3: "Love Letter to Vacation"

I'd like to thank the English Department at Western Michigan University. The kernel of this book was born there with the help of, among others, the following poets, peers, and mentors: Bill Olsen, Nancy Eimers, Jon Adams, Traci Brimhall, Sharon Bryan, Jordan Rice, Andrea England, Chad Sweeney, Jennifer Sweeney, and Adam Clay.

From a distance, via email and phone, these folks are indispensable friends and readers, and I thank them kindly: Keith Montesano, F. Daniel Rzicznek, Amy Newman, Alex Lemon, and Heather Hummel.

Thank you, my Nashville crew: Susan Finch, Tanya Jarrett, Christina Stoddard, Kendra DeColo, Jeff Hardin, Tiana Clark, Susannah Felts, Matt Johnstone, and so many others. Y'all are the best.

Thank you to Eric Fischl, Diane Seuss, Maurice Manning, and Traci Brimhall for their kind words.

Austin Boling. My brother.

Thank you to the *Burnside Review* crew: Sid Miller, for your faith in my work. Dan Kaplan, for helping to shape this book. Shira Richman and Regina Godfrey: thanks as well.

Belmont University and my students: thank you.

Amanda, Auden, Jorie. I love you always.

Gary McDowell is the author of five collections of poetry, including *Mysteries in a World that Thinks There Are None* (Burnside Review Press, 2016), winner of the 2014 Burnside Review Press Book Award; *Weeping at a Stranger's Funeral* (Dream Horse Press, 2014); and *American Amen* (Dream Horse Press, 2010), winner of the 2009 Orphic Prize in Poetry. He's also the co-editor, with F. Daniel Rzicznek, of *The Rose Metal Press Field Guide to Prose Poetry* (Rose Metal Press, 2010). His poems and essays have appeared in *The American Poetry Review*, *The Nation*, *Gulf Coast*, *New England Review*, *Prairie Schooner*, and *Colorado Review*. He lives with his family in Nashville, TN, where he's an assistant professor of English at Belmont University.